The Sideways Planet

Uranus

by Nancy Loewen   illustrated by Jeff Yesh

PICTURE WINDOW BOOKS
Minneapolis, Minnesota

Thanks to our advisers for their expertise, research, and advice:

Lynne Hillenbrand, Ph.D., Professor of Astronomy
California Institute of Technology

Terry Flaherty, Ph.D., Professor of English
Minnesota State University, Mankato

Editor: Jill Kalz
Designers: Amy Muehlenhardt and Melissa Kes
Page Production: Melissa Kes
Art Director: Nathan Gassman
Associate Managing Editor: Christianne Jones
The illustrations in this book were created digitally.

Picture Window Books
A Capstone Imprint
151 Good Counsel Drive
P.O. Box 669
Mankato, MN 56002-0669
877-845-8392
www.capstonepub.com

Printed in the United States of America in North Mankato,
Minnesota.   032010   005743R

All books published by Picture Window Books
are manufactured with paper containing at least
10 percent post-consumer waste.

Library of Congress Cataloging-in-Publication Data
Loewen, Nancy, 1964–
The sideways planet : Uranus / by Nancy Loewen ; illustrated by Jeff Yesh.
p. cm. — (Amazing science. Planets)
Includes index.
ISBN: 978-1-4048-3957-1 (library binding)
ISBN: 978-1-4048-3966-3 (paperback)
1. Uranus (Planet)—Juvenile literature. I. Yesh, Jeff, 1971- ill. II. Title.
QB681.L64 2008
523.47—dc22   2007032881

Table of Contents

It's 1781. In Great Britain, a man named William Herschel
is peering through his telescope. He sees a comet—at least
that's what he thinks it is.

Night after night, he studies the faraway object. Soon he realizes that the object isn't a comet at all. William Herschel has discovered a new planet! It's Uranus, the first planet discovered by using a telescope.

New Ideas

People once believed that there were only six planets. After William Herschel's discovery, they saw that the solar system was much bigger than they had imagined.

Uranus is 1.8 billion miles (2.9 billion kilometers) away from the sun. It is twice as far from the sun as its nearest neighbor, Saturn. And it is 19 times as far away from the sun as Earth!

Jupiter

Uranus

Neptune

Saturn

Mercury

Venus

Earth

Mars

FUN FACT
Of our solar system's eight planets—Mercury, Venus, Earth, Mars, Jupiter, Saturn, Uranus, and Neptune—Uranus is the seventh planet from the sun.

EDITOR'S NOTE
In this illustration, the distances between planets are not to scale. In reality, the distances between the outer planets are much greater than the distances between the inner planets.

A Gas Giant

Uranus is made mostly of gas, not rock. It is one of the gas giant planets. The other gas giants are Jupiter, Saturn, and Neptune.

Like the other gas giants, Uranus is huge. Its diameter is more than four times the diameter of Earth. Uranus is the third-largest planet in our solar system. Only Jupiter and Saturn are bigger.

FUN FACT
In Greek mythology, Uranus was the first god of the sky, the ruler of the heavens.

Earth

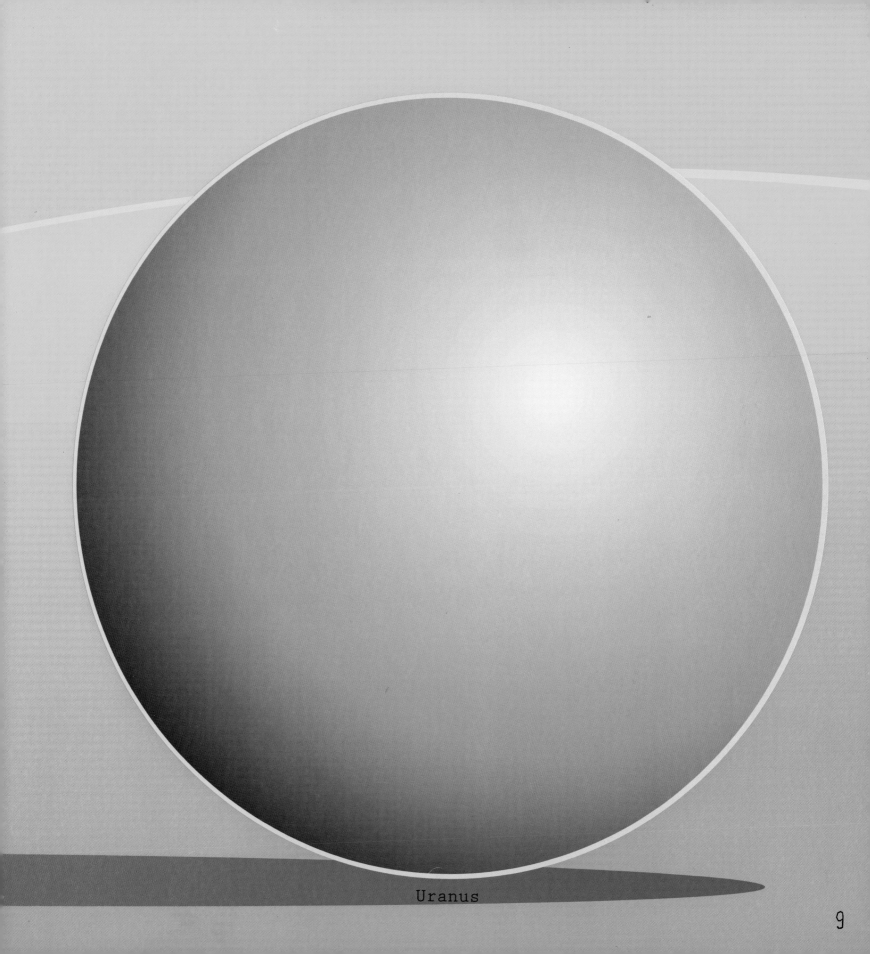

Uranus

9

Under Pressure

Uranus does not have a solid surface. It is made mostly of gas—mostly hydrogen and helium.

The weight of Uranus' atmosphere pushes inward, toward the planet's center. This pushing is called atmospheric pressure. Gases are pressed together more and more tightly the nearer they are to the center. The gases get so tightly pressed that they turn into liquid.

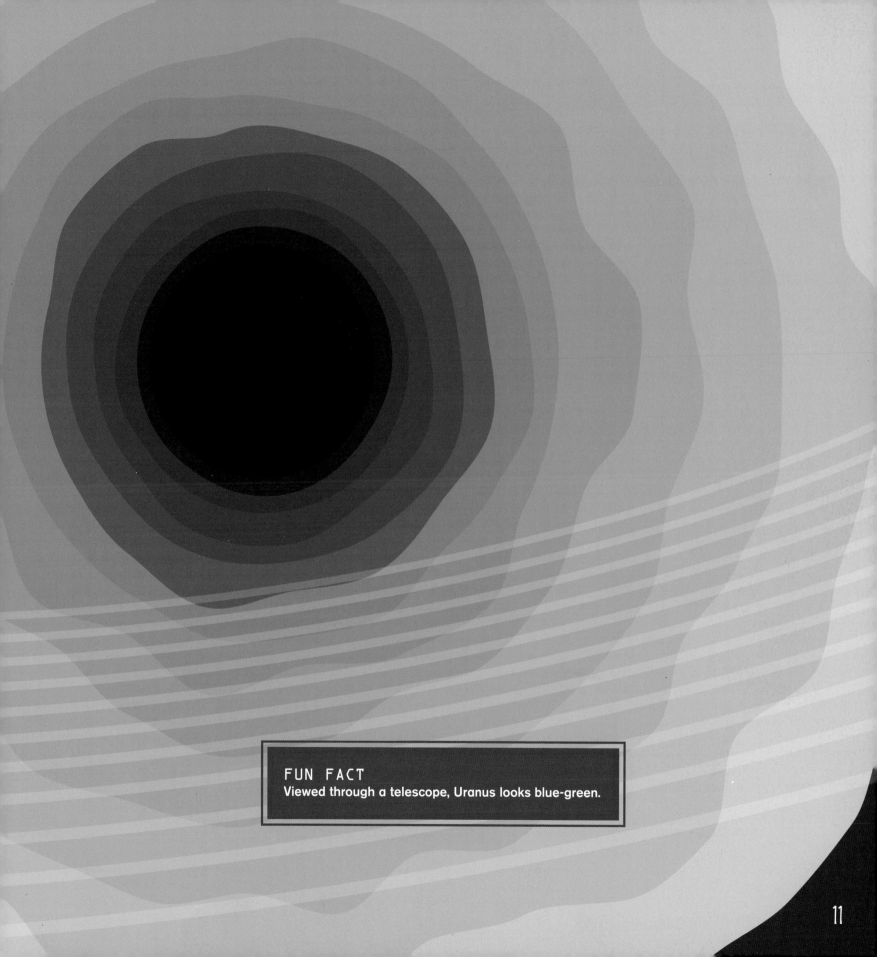

FUN FACT
Viewed through a telescope, Uranus looks blue-green.

Hot and Cold

Because Uranus is so far away, it gets very little heat from the sun. It is often called an ice giant. The average temperature of Uranus' atmosphere is minus 350 degrees Fahrenheit (minus 212 degrees Celsius).

Inside the planet, however, temperatures reach more than 12,000 F (6,654 C). So why doesn't the liquid boil away?

1.8 billion miles (2.9 billion km) from the sun

The same pressure that squeezes the gases together also keeps the liquid from boiling. Deep within Uranus, the pressure is five million times stronger than it is at sea level on Earth!

°F 12,000 °C 6,654

°F °C
-350 -212

FUN FACT
Strong winds circle around Uranus. They can reach speeds of up to 450 miles (720 km) per hour.

The Sideways Planet

Uranus is tilted so far on its axis that it looks like it's sideways! If Earth were tilted that much, its north and south poles would be where its equator is now.

Many scientists think that a planet-sized object hit Uranus when the solar system was newly formed. The impact knocked Uranus on its side, and it has stayed in that position ever since.

FUN FACT
Because of Uranus' strange position, scientists sometimes disagree on just which pole is north and which is south!

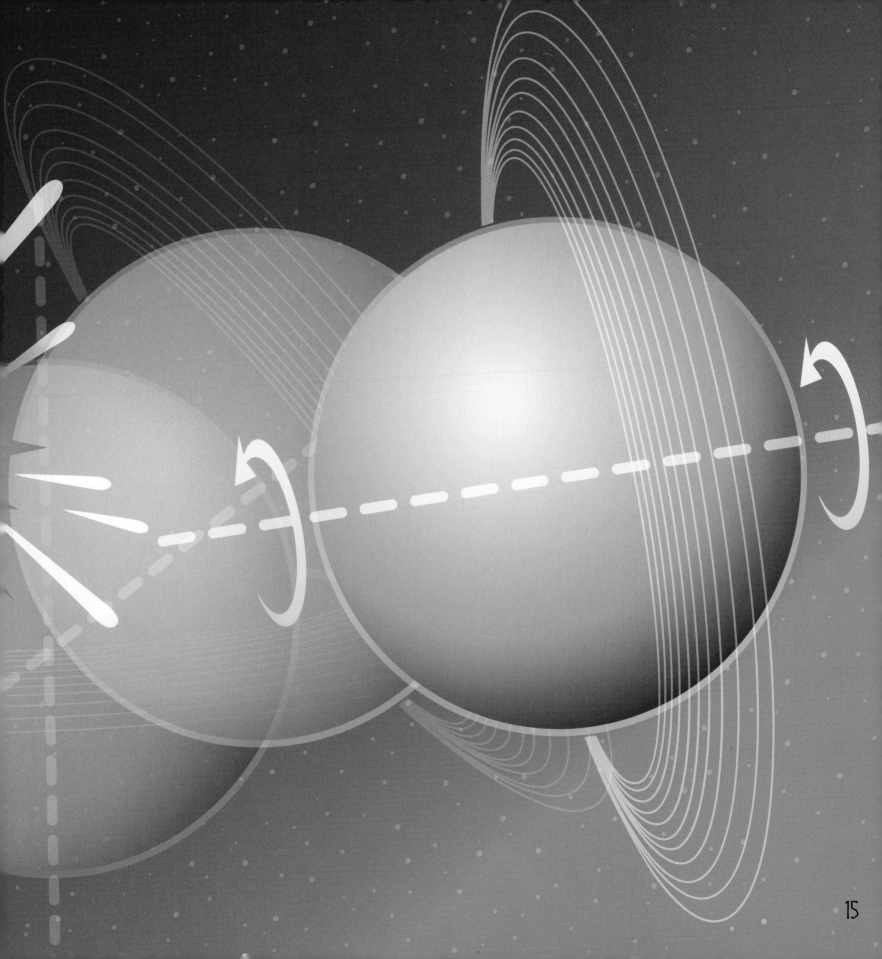

Days and Years

On Uranus, a day is short, but a year is really, really long.

A day is the amount of time a planet takes to spin on its axis one time. On Uranus, a day lasts about 18 Earth hours. On Earth, a day lasts 24 hours.

FUN FACT
Uranus is one of only two planets (Venus is the other) to spin in a clockwise direction.

A year is the amount of time a planet takes to orbit once
around the sun. One year on Uranus takes 84 Earth years!

Strange Seasons

Uranus' sideways tilt and its long year cause unusual seasons. For half of the planet's orbit, the north pole points toward the sun. It has 42 Earth years of sunlight. But when the north pole points away from the sun, it has 42 Earth years of darkness.

Moons and Rings

Uranus is not alone on its long journey around the sun. At least 27 moons orbit the planet. Uranus is also circled by 11 rings. The rings are made up of dust and pieces of rock and ice.

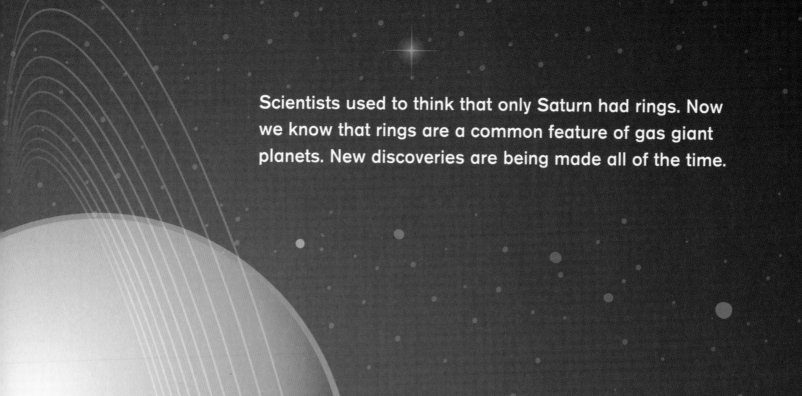

Scientists used to think that only Saturn had rings. Now we know that rings are a common feature of gas giant planets. New discoveries are being made all of the time.

FUN FACT
Many of Uranus' moons are named for characters in William Shakespeare's plays. Examples include Puck and Titania, from "A Midsummer Night's Dream," and Juliet, from "Romeo and Juliet."

Stepping Out in Space

Astronomers measure the huge distances in space using "astronomical units." One astronomical unit (AU) is equal to 93 million miles (149 million km). This is the average distance between Earth and the sun.

In this activity, the length of your foot will stand for one astronomical unit.

What you need:
• four balls or other objects you can use as markers
• a place where there's plenty of room to spread out

What you do:

1. Put one marker on the ground. This marker is the sun.

2. Put the edge of your heel in front of the sun. Place another marker in front of your toe. This marker is Earth.

3. Now, put your heel in front of Earth. Take your other foot and place it at your toe. Keep moving your feet in a straight line, heel to toe. After nine steps, stop. Put down your third marker at about the middle of your foot. This marker is Saturn.

4. Put your heel in front of your toe and start over with your counting. Stop when you get to 10. Put down your last marker. You've arrived at Uranus!

See how close Earth is to the sun, compared to the other two planets? See how the discovery of Uranus doubled the size of our solar system? (And Neptune, which was discovered later, is even farther out!)

Fun Facts

- Uranus can be pronounced two ways: YOOR-eh-nehs or yoo-RAY-nehs.

- Other astronomers had seen Uranus before William Herschel did. But they thought it was a star.

- Uranus travels through space at an average speed of more than 15,000 miles (24,000 km) per hour.

- Because Uranus is so far away, only one spacecraft has visited the planet. *Voyager 2* passed by in 1986.

- The gravity on Uranus is about 88 percent of Earth's gravity. If you weigh 100 pounds (45 kilograms) on Earth, you would weigh 88 pounds (40 kg) on Uranus.

Glossary

astronomer—a scientist who studies stars, planets, and other objects in space

atmosphere—the gases that surround a planet

axis—the center on which something spins, or rotates

comet—an icy ball that orbits the sun

diameter—the distance of a line running from one side of a circle, through the center, and across to the other side

equator—an imaginary line around the center of a planet, between the north and south poles

gravity—the force that pulls things down toward the surface of a planet

orbit—the path an object takes to travel around a star or planet; also, to travel around a star or planet

solar system—the sun and the bodies that orbit around it; these bodies include planets, dwarf planets, asteroids, and comets

telescope—a device with mirrors or lenses; a telescope makes faraway objects appear closer

To Learn More

More Books to Read

Howard, Fran. *Uranus.* Edina, Minn.: ABDO Pub. Co., 2008.
Landau, Elaine. *Uranus.* New York: Children's Press, 2008.
Rau, Dana Meachen. *Uranus.* Minneapolis: Compass Point Books, 2003.
Ring, Susan. *Uranus.* New York: Weigl Publishers, 2004.

On the Web

FactHound offers a safe, fun way to find Web sites related to topics in this book.
All of the sites on FactHound have been researched by our staff.

1. Visit *www.facthound.com*
2. Type in this special code: 1404839577
3. Click on the FETCH IT button.

Your trusty FactHound will fetch the best sites for you!

Index

Look for all of the books in the Amazing Science: Planets series: